HELP YOUR KIDS STAY
DRUG-FREE

HELP YOUR KIDS STAY DRUG-FREE

PAUL FRANCIS

HarperCollins*Publishers*

HarperCollins*Publishers*
77–85 Fulham Palace Road, London W6 8JB
www.fireandwater.com

First published in Great Britain in 1999 by HarperCollins*Publishers*

1 3 5 7 9 10 8 6 4 2

Paul Francis asserts the moral right to be identified
as the author of this work

A catalogue record for this book is available from the British Library

ISBN 0 00 274038 9

Printed and bound in Great Britain by
Caledonian International Book Publishing Ltd, Glasgow

To Sue and Neil

CONTENTS

ACKNOWLEDGEMENTS

I found this a very difficult book to write and I am therefore very grateful to friends whose encouragement and advice kept me going. The first and final drafts of this book are astonishingly different, thanks mainly to the feedback from these friends.

My thanks go to Steve Gardiner, Sharon Chapman and Pat Brooks for their very helpful comments and insights on the manuscript. I'm also thankful for the research done by Andy Pantling.

Thanks also to my good friend Rob Parsons, who knows a lot about writing and, as always, was kind enough to share his knowledge and time to help me.

One poor lady, Caroline Adams, had the unenviable job of reading a number of the drafts to correct my poor use of English. Anyone who has the patience to do that deserves my gratitude.

Special thanks to Daniel Adams for showing me around his room and opening a door on youth culture.

A 'thank-you' must also go to the rehabilitation and education centres that I visited when looking into the whole issue of drug abuse. They do a great job and society owes them a great deal of gratitude.

Thanks go to my editor, Elspeth Taylor, who has, among many essential qualities, one in particular – she can change deadlines! Much of an editor's work is often hidden, but it is much appreciated.

A final, very deep sense of gratitude goes to all the team I have the privilege of working with. Without their patience, understanding and help I doubt this book would have been written.

INTRODUCTION: THE CAR RAMP

I have worked for many years with young people, but my original profession was civil engineering. I did this for only two years, but in that time I worked on various projects and learned a number of lessons. My first and probably greatest lesson was experienced when I worked on a multi-storey car park. The car park was designed to have six floors, with access to these via a circular ramp that spiralled up the side of the building. My job was to build that ramp. Of course, the first stage in any building work is the foundations. For the ramp these needed to be big and deep, measuring about 10 metres square and 15 metres deep. I marked out where the hole was to be and got the appropriate machine to dig it. I then ordered the concrete. On the morning the wagons were due to start delivering the concrete, the site manager approached me and simply asked, 'Are you confident that this hole is in the right place?' With all the confidence and assurance of a young person I replied, 'Of course!' As first truck with the concrete arrived, I caught sight of the site manager and the senior engineer frantically scampering round the hole. After ten minutes, a very agitated site manager stormed towards me and, in language I could not repeat, basically told me that the foundation hole was in the wrong place – not by millimetres or centimetres, but by 20 metres! Needless to say, the concrete was stopped, the hole filled in and another re-dug. I'm still convinced it would have been the best ramp ever built – the only problem was that it would have ended up taking cars into thin air!

As you can imagine, I do not regard that as one of the highlights of my career. But the lesson it did teach me was the incredible importance of foundations. They're essential to buildings.

Why do I start with this story? Simply put, foundations may be essential to buildings, but they are also vital to our personal lives and to society at large. The past 30 years have seen a large increase in the illegal drug industry, so that today drug and alcohol abuse is a major problem in our modern culture. It is among the issues that create great fear and concern for parents. Images of your child connected to a life-support machine haunt the mind. Parties where you have no idea what is going on and what is being given out.

How can we ensure that our children remain drug-free? We have had many very good campaigns to try to educate young people about the dangers. But whatever the success of these campaigns, the problem is still increasing. The purpose of this book is to help you take a step back and ask some questions. What can I do that will help my child stay drug-free? What do I need to equip them with, so that they know how to deal with the issues before they're confronted by them? How can we create a framework that gives our children the best opportunity to stand against the tide and say no to drugs?

There are no easy answers to these questions, but we need to make a start. I have written *Help Your Kids Stay*

Drug-Free for that very reason – recognizing that it will be difficult but that there are some things we can begin to do that will help. This book is not written as an ABC on drugs and their effects – there are already plenty of excellent books on the topic. Rather, I try to look at what happens before the drugs are offered. Some of you are young parents with young children, and you want to give it your best shot at helping them. Some of you are simply despairing about what to do. I hope that the goals I write about will help you.

I have tried to give some guidelines and life-skills that will help us to lay foundations to give our children a fighting chance of staying drug-free. The *1:00 Hour Survival Guide* is a short book. It is written to be read in an hour. There are three sections. The first looks at why young people take drugs. The second is a set of six goals to help you, as a parent, to help your children. The third and final set of six goals is there to help you, as a parent, cope with it all. At regular intervals there are 'Time out' pages which sum up what has gone before and 'Action' pages containing some simple points that I hope will help. The book is written to be read from the beginning, but you can always dip in wherever you want. I hope it helps you.

**People who feel good about themselves
will have a much better chance of
coping with life**

GOAL 1

TO UNDERSTAND WHY YOUNG PEOPLE TAKE DRUGS

At the end of our schools presentations on drugs I always leave time for the pupils to ask questions. For me this is always great, because you are never really sure what to expect. There is, however, one question we always get asked: 'Tell me, if drugs are so bad, how come so many people take them?' A very good question, and one that most young people will ask at some point. For parents, the questions are different: 'Why my son? Why my daughter? Why does anybody take drugs?'

These are very good questions, and so in the next two chapters I want to try to help you understand why young people take drugs. If we can manage to do this, then we will have a chance of helping our children to say no to drug and alcohol abuse. To help, in this chapter I have written about four different situations. They are events that take place every day in countless towns throughout our country. I make no moral judgement, but simply use them to help you begin to enter into your youngster's world.

A NICE LAD

John was an average 16-year-old. He passed most of his exams every year, and his reports maybe had one A, a couple of Bs, mostly Cs and the odd D. If you asked the teachers about him they would have to think for a second, and then they would say something like, 'Oh, John! Yes, he's a nice lad. Quiet, though – tends to keep himself to himself.' He has neither enemies nor any real friends. He is not the last to be picked for teams – but neither is he the first. All his school mates think he's OK and they don't mind him joining them as long as he stays in the background. If you were to take a straw poll of people who know him, they would say that he seems a fairly happy person.

But John has a secret – or should I say a need? He wants to be liked – no more than that. He would do anything to be the life and the soul of the party. Nothing would give him greater pleasure than for his mates to laugh at his jokes, for people to leave with him when he moves from one club to another. He would love the women to flirt with him, and when they are at the rave for them to be dancing round him. Nothing would give him greater pleasure – because it would tell him that people really do like him, that he is valued and loved. But John knows that isn't going to happen.

One evening when he was at one of the clubs, one of his mates came up to him and simply said, 'John, you really need to loosen up a bit. Here, try this,' and offered him an Ecstasy tablet. John does not know why he took it. He knew all the dangers – he had decided a couple of years back that only idiots did drugs. But, for whatever reason, he took it. It transformed his evening – he loved everybody, everything became so cool, and everyone became his friend. For the first time in his life he felt that he belonged, that he had arrived.

A DAY OUT OF SCHOOL

Andy, Tom and Rob never got on at school. They made it through year 9, but in year 10 they began the process of not bothering to go in. At first it was fun, a morning in the town centre, afternoon in the cinema. But that soon got boring and they looked around for things to do. It was Tom who brought the carrier bag back; as he walked towards Andy and Rob they gave each other a quizzical look, because Tom seemed drunk. His eyes were glazed and he could not stand upright but swayed from side to side. 'Try some,' he said, shoving the bag in front of their faces. They both looked inside and saw the substance. 'No way,' said Andy, 'it does your brains in.' But Rob took another look, said, 'Not much else to do,' stuck his nose in, and began.

They found his body on the pavement at the base of an eight-storey car park. When Tom came out of his 'high' he could only remember snatches. His story came out in bursts between the tears. Rob, it seemed, took a lot of sniffs and began to talk about 'Batman' and 'flying'. He ran up the car park, laughing and shouting about 'the Joker'. When they reached the top he didn't stop: he simply ran to the edge, shouting and laughing that Batman could fly. Tom can still hear the laugh and scream as he went over the edge.

IBIZA

Jane, Claire, Ann and Jo had saved up all year. It was Friday night and they waited excitedly at Luton Airport for the 11.00 p.m. flight to Ibiza. For the last six months they had talked about nothing else to their mates. The fun, the clubs, the booze, the men! They had only one thing on their mind. For 8 hours a day, 5 days a week, 50 weeks a year, life was tedious, boring and monotonous. This was their chance of fun, of getting away from it all and just going simply and utterly wild. It was going to be great! They landed in Ibiza at 3.00 a.m. and arrived at the apartment at 4.30. After a few hours' sleep, they all woke at around 2.00 p.m., and the fun began. Bacardi, rum, whatever took their fancy. By early evening they were 'tanked up'. On the streets they knew what to look for and, sure enough, after only 30 minutes they found him. A bit more expensive than they thought, £15 a pill, but this was holiday time!

As they entered the club the music beat dug deep into their bodies. They looked at one another, smiled, and each 'popped' a pill. Let the party begin!

THE BREAKDOWN

Mary knew that, early on, her parents tried to keep it quiet. They would wait until she was in bed before they started. At first it was just harsh words which she could just make out, followed by long silences. But as the weeks passed her parents' words got louder, and soon they were shouting and occasionally throwing things at one another. It was, of course, her fault, she told herself. If only she was a better daughter they would love one another. She tried harder, but nothing changed – in fact it got worse. So for the past month she had ended up crying herself to sleep. She had never felt so alone in the world.

One day her friend caught her crying in the toilet at school. And before she knew it, everything had come out. Her friend was pretty matter-of-fact about it and told her the same thing had happened to her.

'But what about the pain?' Mary asked. 'How did you cope with that?'

'Oh, like you I cried a lot. But then somebody told me to try this.' With that she rolled up her sleeves and showed Mary the marks.

'Did it help?' asked Mary.

'You bet!' her friend said. With that she pulled out a tin and, tapping the lid, said, 'Bye-bye pain.' Mary only hesitated for a second: she rolled up her sleeve, looked at her friend, and said, 'Help me.'

A year later Mary is mainlining and selling her body to pay for it. The pain has gone, but so has every other feeling. 'The living dead' is how she described it to one person.

Four different people in very different situations, but they all took drugs for the same reason – THEY WORKED. Whatever their need – boredom, fun, pain – they saw that taking the drug provided the answer. This is the hardest truth for us to understand or accept, but we must if we want to do something about the problem. The reason young people take drugs is because they work. For young people the benefit of taking drugs outweighs the potential risk factor. If we can understand and believe this, we are at the start of sorting out a solution.

But hang on in there: in the next chapter we will look at this issue in more detail.

**Drugs are not a problem to young people.
They are the answers to the problem
of life**

My life was such a torment that I actually felt like killing myself. I used to drive home in my car and seriously think, 'Should I pull over in front of this lorry?' It got that bad. I hit rock bottom and couldn't handle it anymore.

Paul Merson, international footballer [1]

GOAL 2

TO UNDERSTAND MORE ABOUT WHY YOUNG PEOPLE TAKE DRUGS

If you are still struggling with the concepts in the last chapter, let me try to help you by posing a question. If you have a headache, what do you do? Most of us would take a paracetamol because we know that they work. If a person has an infection the doctor will often give antibiotics – and they will work. If someone is clinically depressed and is given medication, there is every chance that the drugs will help the person. Drugs in medicine will, by and large, work. It is generally the same with recreational drugs. Your son and daughter are now living in a culture which says, 'If you want a good time, one way is to take drugs.' If they are going through major pain there are drugs which, for a few hours, will take it away. Make no mistake, there is more pain in our world: bullying, anorexia nervosa, suicides and attempted suicides are all rising, a clear indicator that we have created a tortured culture. So drugs really do ...

- help blank out the pain of loneliness
- relieve the emptiness of being or feeling unloved
- make you feel more sociable when you feel embarrassed and tongue-tied
- make you feel accepted when you have always felt a failure
- make you feel adequate when you have always felt inadequate.

TWO MAJOR PROBLEMS

I have majored on this point because it is important that we understand it. However, there are two problems which are the reasons we need to keep young people off drugs. The first is the other side of the story. Visit any hospital on any day and you will discover patients with direct or indirect drug- and alcohol-related conditions. One in every four male general hospital beds is occupied by someone whose health has been affected by alcohol. You will find teenagers with Ecstasy-related illnesses. Young people do not see this side. A major part we have to play is to give them this information and help them to understand that it could be them in the hospital bed.

Second, and more important, drugs only work for a short period of time. If you regularly take speed you will find that the buzz does not last as long as it used to, and to get the same effect you will need to take more. To help you understand why they only work for a short period, let me tell you about a day out.

A DAY AT ALTON TOWERS

A while ago I took some young people to Alton Towers. As we drove, there was talk about only one thing: Nemesis. For those who have not been to Alton Towers, Nemesis is a ride that is guaranteed to 'scare you to death'. Just looking at it made me feel sick! All the way, Nemesis was the talk of the group. There was a real buzz and excitement about it.

We arrived, and queued for over an hour just to get on the ride. As I looked at the group I could tell they were afraid: they tried to hide it, but their white faces said it all. However, when they finished the ride it was a different story – they were so high that we had to pull them down. At that point they felt they were kings for a day. If I had challenged them to do anything they would have done it, because they were so high, they felt so good. They went on the ride for a second time. This time they did not look so white, they were a bit more relaxed – after all, they had done this before. When they came off they didn't look so green. But also they weren't quite as high as after the first ride. If they had gone on it a third, fourth and fifth time, there would have been a diminishing return of the 'high factor'. Before long they would have been looking for the next new ride to give them that initial buzz. That's the way the human body is designed – it can give a buzz for a certain length of time, but then needs more to create the same effect.

The body is a marvellous creation, but it is designed to function in certain ways. In very simple terms, drugs work because they stimulate parts of the body or brain. But two things happen. First, for a while the drug will have its desired effect, but very quickly you will need more of the same to create the effect. And second, if you keep overloading the body, in the end it simply packs in and dies.

This is why it's important that young people have all the facts and life-skills to make the 'right' decisions. There are a number of other reasons why young people take drugs, and they are highlighted on the next page.

TIME OUT

Ten reasons why young people take drugs

- to rebel or to shock people
- to feel they belong to a group of friends
- because they want to take risks
- because it's fun
- because it's the 'in' thing to do
- because it's part of a night out – maybe at a rave
- because it feels and looks grown-up
- because they're bored
- because drugs are easy to get hold of
- BECAUSE THEY WORK

Suicide is Britain's second biggest killer among young people. In 1995, 19 per cent of deaths in the 15- to 24-year-old group were suicides.[2]

SIX GOALS TO HELP PARENTS HELP YOUNG PEOPLE

A VERY IMPORTANT PAGE

I have deliberately started the book with two chapters on why young people take drugs. For you to have any chance of helping your children, you must take on board what was said. Having accepted that any young person could take drugs, we are now in a position to look at some of the frameworks our young people need to survive.

Young people need information and facts about drugs and alcohol to help them in their decision-making choices. But they need more than that. They need skills to help them cope with life. In fact, I would go as far as saying that the skills are more essential than the facts. For if they have the skills to cope with life, there is a strong chance that they will stay drug-free. That is why this book is not full of information about types of drugs and their effects. There are already plenty of good books on that subject. Rather, in writing this book I have tried to go back to the foundations. We need to equip our young people to cope with life. They need to have skills to solve problems when confronted with them, to recognize the power of peer pressure and to see the value of friendship. The next few chapters will look at some of these issues in detail.

GOAL 3

TO UNDERSTAND THE GREATEST FORCE SHAPING YOUNG PEOPLE

As we begin to tackle the problem, we need to ask our-selves a simple question: if more money and time has been put into drug education in the past few years than ever before, why then is the problem getting worse? This is not to say that the money has been badly spent or that the education is not good. Rather, it's to recognize that we have failed to face and tackle the greatest problem in the battle against drug use. To help us look at the issue let me take you to a school playground.

It's 3.30 p.m. on an autumn afternoon. Annie's mother is standing by the school gate with all the other mothers and fathers as they wait for the end-of-school bell to ring. The conversation is on the normal things parents talk about – their children's sniffles and coughs, the problem with secondary school, the new music teacher, and so on. The bell finally goes and the children stream out of the door. Annie's mother can't spot her at once, but then she sees her. She has long blonde hair which this week is tied up in a ponytail. As Annie runs towards the gate her mother feels her heart leap. She is so pleased with her 8-year-old daughter. Listening to the other mothers' and fathers' conversation, she realizes that everything is working out so well. She knows there is no such thing as a perfect daughter, but Annie has to be close. And as they walk off down the street, hand in hand, Annie talking about her school day, her mother thinks to herself, 'I love my life and my daughter.'

Let me take you ten years down the road. Annie is now 18, and again her mother is standing waiting. But this time it's not outside a school gate, but rather by a hospital bed, for in that bed, connected to a life-support machine, lies her daughter. As the doctors monitor the machine, Annie's mother's mind is filled with questions: 'Why did she take the Ecstasy tablet? Why my daughter? How did I fail her as a parent?'

Ten years, and what a change. Had Annie simply turned into a difficult teenager? Was her mother a bad parent? The answer to both these questions is no. But I use this story to illustrate what is probably one of the greatest and most powerful influences on your children. The pressure begins from about the age of 9 or 10, and really builds up into the teenage years. The pressure – peer pressure, the pressure from their friends. I can't overestimate the strength of this.

IT'S NOT JUST YOUNG PEOPLE – IT'S ALL OF US

Walk into the Stock Exchange and notice how many people are wearing jeans and a sweatshirt. I would suggest that there will be none. The reason for this is simple – everybody is wearing a designer suit and braces. Why? Because *everybody* is wearing one. In other words, it's the pressure of the group. If you don't believe me, check out the car park of an expensive golf club – will you find any second-hand Escorts? I doubt it. Why? Because everybody is driving an expensive car. What I'm saying is that the pressure of our peers is very strong. I bought a suit for the first time last week. Before that, if I went to any function that was meant to be 'smart', I would wear a jacket and trousers. However, if everybody else was wearing a suit I felt uncomfortable, I did not feel I belonged. That is the strength of peer pressure. Unless you conform, it can make you feel that you don't belong. At the heart of each one of us is a real sense of wanting to belong – a real sense of identifying with and belonging to a community.

If it is strong for adults, imagine the power it has on young people. It moulds them to want to stay part of the group. It can make them do things they know are wrong, but the pressure is too great. It is summed up by a letter in the *Daily Mirror* newspaper about the age and reason why a young girl had sex for the first time.

... we started kissing and cuddling and one thing led to another. I had hoped it would be very special – you know, very romantic. I imagined that it would be something out of a film with music and flowers. Unfortunately it was over very quickly and I just thought: is that it? I was shocked that I had actually gone through with it and became very tearful ... It sounds so obvious now but at the time I hadn't thought hard about it. Naïvely I just wanted to be part of the gang who had done it. The next day when I went to school my friends asked: 'Have you done it yet?' I pretended that it had been a great experience and they were very proud of me and made me feel part of the gang. But I felt as if I had done something wrong and in my heart I wished I hadn't gone through with it. But as far as my friends were concerned, I was now one of them.[3]

As young people enter the adolescent years their emotions climb all over the place. In that emotional battlefield the desire to belong to a group is huge. It is so big that the young person will listen to their friend's voice more than your voice. It is why I feel so passionate against football teams that constantly change strips, because they work on peer-group pressure. If your child is the only one not to have the new strip, they will do everything to get it – which means they will nag you for it. Advertisers and manufacturers cynically manipulate this group-pressure dynamic. It reminds me of a documentary about Nike, where a number of young people in London were interviewed and asked one question: 'Don't you mind being exploited by paying £120 for trainers that only cost about £25 to make?' Their answers show the power of peer pressure. 'Yes, we do mind being exploited, but it's the fashion, so we will pay the money.' Do you see the irony of it all? Who's made it fashion? Two groups: the advertisers, and their friends. It's only because their friends have them that they want to wear them.

So when a young person is with a group of friends and they all start smoking, what is he to do? When friends start smoking cannabis, what is she to do? When they are at the rave and they all are taking speed, what does she or he say? Your child's desire to belong to the group, to keep his friends, is an enormous influence. But don't give up, because I believe that there are frameworks we can put into our young people's lives which will help them to withstand even this great pressure.

Most youths who smoke tobacco are making conscious decisions to be with a peer group dominated by smokers.[4]

The majority of addicts were first introduced to drugs by their friends.

TIME OUT

Seven signs of a person with a healthy self-esteem

- They have a balanced view of who they are; they know their strengths as well as their weaknesses.

- Knowing the first point means they will be able to recognize the truth about themselves when other people point it out.

- Their sense of value is not too strongly dependent on what people think.

- They are prepared to speak truth as they see it, without fear of rejection and with no intent to harm others.

- They are trustworthy and reliable.

- They are happy to be part of the crowd but not necessarily to follow just because everybody else is.

- They are happy to see others doing well.

GOAL 4

TO HELP YOUNG PEOPLE COPE WITH PEER PRESSURE

So the pressure from their friends is enormous. It will take a lot of work to help our young people – but it is possible. There are a number of foundations we can build into our children's lives which will give them a fighting chance of resisting that pressure. The first and most important one is to help your son or daughter develop a healthy self-esteem. Self-esteem is what we think of ourselves. If we achieve this, it does not mean that they won't have any problems, or will cause you fewer tears. But what it does mean is that it should free them from doing or achieving things simply to be liked by others. It's one of the strongest weapons you can give your child to cope with the pressure from their peers. We have just looked at seven traits of a person with healthy self-esteem. I believe there are four foundations we can give our children which will help them in developing this healthy self-esteem.

FOUNDATION A: GIVE THEM UNCONDITIONAL LOVE

I sometimes visit a special needs school. It is a great school with around 120 children with severe disabilities. I visited their assembly on prize-giving day – but this was prize-giving of a different kind. The hall was packed with the children and one or two parents who had come to watch what was taking place. I sat at the back next to a 75-year-old woman whom I did not know. The headmaster began, 'Mary, you have won a prize for holding a knife and fork for the first time.' Mary, a 14-year-old, was wheeled forward to collect her prize. As she did so, John, a lad with Down's Syndrome standing at the back, applauded her all the way to the front and back again. 'Peter,' went on the headmaster, 'you managed to walk in a straight line this week, come and collect your prize.' As he walked forward, almost in a straight line, John applauded him all the way. This extraordinary celebration of human achievement went on – prize after prize was given, and each time John would applaud the person. Finally, the headmaster said, 'John, you did a good piece of artwork this week. Come and collect your prize.' With that, John went to collect his prize – and applauded himself! As he went forward the old woman next to me, who till this point had been very quiet, sat up straight. She nudged me in the ribs and turned to look at me. With a broad smile and tears falling down her face, she pointed towards John and simply said, 'That is my grandson.' I knew nothing about John, but one thing I learned that morning is that he was loved. John has many difficulties and will have many hurdles to over-come in life, but one thing is clear: he knows he is loved, and that will make all the difference.

Give your child that same demonstration of love, for it is critical to their self-esteem. I'm sure you don't mean it, but is your affection greater when they pass exams, wear the clothes you are happy with and mix with your choice of friends? If this is true, then your children will learn that your love is conditional. And the child who learns this will be more insecure. This will contribute to them looking elsewhere for acceptance and love. This desire to be accepted by their friends will probably override any other skill, for one simple reason: they want to be loved and they will equate this with pleasing their friends, so they will do what they tell them. Let your children know you love them – whatever they do or achieve.

FOUNDATION B: BUILD THEM UP

A friend of mine, Adam Jones, was about to leave for work. It was his first day in work, his first job. Last week he'd finished school, now it was work. His stomach was tight with nerves – he felt very frightened. As he walked out of the door, his father shouted from the kitchen, 'Remember, son, when you walk on to the factory floor: you're Adam Jones.' It lifted my friend's heart. Why? Because his father had reminded him of a fundamental truth: you are a unique creation, so don't let anybody put you down. Encourage your child to believe that they are a unique and wonderful creation.

I remember reading about someone who said they wished they were like Richard Branson. The reply was quick, 'Why stoop to be lower than you are?' Now what the person was trying to communicate is that you are unique; to want to be someone else is to be less than you are. The point is not a criticism of Richard Branson, for the same could be said of him if he wished to be someone else. Your child is unique, so tell them to be themselves.

FOUNDATION C: TEACH THEM THE VALUE OF POSITIVE CRITICISM

Learn to take criticism, for it will help you to grow. One of the big lessons we all need to learn is that we have many failings. The secret is not to deny these, but to be open to people who gently point them out. I can appear impatient at times. On occasions, people have approached me and told me that I upset them the other day when I cut them off in mid-sentence. I could react in one of two ways, either denying it or saying something like, 'I know. I'm sorry, it's a weakness of mine that I'm working on.' The latter is a much healthier way to live. Gently encourage your children that positive criticism can be a good thing.

FOUNDATION D: HELP THEM TO BE KIND TO OTHERS

When I was in school we had to spend an afternoon doing community service. One of the tasks I did was to visit old people in hospital. I remember visiting an old lady. When told that we were visiting people who had no visitors that day, she burst into tears. After she had calmed down, she told me that nobody visited her and how much better she felt just for seeing me. Now that did two things: it made her feel better and it made me feel good! We would do well to help our children to help and be kind to others. To break down the effects of a very self-absorbed culture will be hard, but one of the ways is to create in your children a desire to help others.

Having established a sense of security and well-being in our children we will also need to equip them with skills to help them through life. This is tackled in the next two chapters.

ACTION POINTS

- Spend five minutes looking at the influence your friends have on your life.

- Think of five ways in which you are able to say no to your friends without causing offence.

- List five drugs and the effects they have.

- If you can't do the above, pick up a leaflet on drugs and read it.

TIME OUT

Four ways to build up your child's self-esteem

- Love them for who they are, not what they achieve.

- Every day tell them at least one positive thing they have done.

- Let them see the value of positive criticism in your life.

- Encourage them to be kind to people.

One of the major reasons why young people take drugs is to avoid pain. Part of the reason they take them is that it's the only way they know to cope with the pain. However, what we want to do is give our children life skills which show there are other ways of coping with difficulties.

GOAL 5

TO TEACH YOUR CHILDREN THE ESSENTIAL LIFE-SKILLS

As we saw in the last chapter, having a healthy self-esteem is a major weapon in fighting the influence of peer pressure. That, however, is only a starting point, for we can go on helping our young people cope with all the pressure of modern life by giving them life-skills. In short, these are skills which help them to make 'good' decisions. We need to give them skills so that, when faced with a problem, they will either know how to deal with it or have the knowledge to work out what to do. This, I appreciate, is not easy, but it is possible.

To do this we need to give our young people life-skills that help their self-esteem, that enable them to make 'good' decisions under pressure and to work out what is of real value in life. I see that there are three life-skills we need to share with them.

LIFE-SKILL 1: HELPING YOUNG PEOPLE TO KNOW WHAT THEY BELIEVE

When I was at college a friend of mine, on graduating, was offered a job with a major oil company. He, along with all the new employees, was flown up to Aberdeen for an induction weekend. Over 200 of them gathered for an opening meal in one of the top hotels. At the end of the meal a number of managers gave some short speeches.

Finally, the managing director stood up and said this: 'Welcome to ... We have employed you because you are the best in your field. But at this moment you need to realize a truth. The company you now work for is your god. You will serve it night and day, and you can have no other god but us. If you have trouble with this you had better walk out now.'

My friend tells me that nobody did walk out. But the point is simple: if you had not worked out the answer to the question by then, it was too late. The reason I say this is because by that age you have consciously or subconsciously learned what your core values to life are. These will then be reflected in how you live. If making more money and climbing high in a company were high value, then you would not walk out. If, however, family life, healthy living, treating other people with dignity were high value, then you would have to ask yourself some big questions. Help your children to work this out in the 'good' times, because you can't work it out under pressure. I see three steps in achieving this.

Step A: Identify the core values of what you believe

I believe there are some core issues where we need to have values that we must pass on to our children. Not to have a value is to make a statement, and our children learn from it. These are what I consider to be core values:

- your views on authority
- your views on God and spirituality
- your attitude towards health
- your views on sexuality
- the way you treat other people
- your attitude towards money and possessions
- your attitude towards power
- knowing right from wrong
- the way you deal with pain and difficulties.

Some would argue that this is a bit naïve. How can you pass these values on? But this is exactly my point – everybody passes on their values. The fact that we may not be aware we're doing it is not the issue, for they will be passed on. What I am arguing, for your children's sake, is that you think about what you consider to be of value and what you want to pass on. To give an example of what I mean, take the core value 'knowing right from wrong'.

I believe that we have to teach them that there is right and wrong. A generation that has brought children up with relative values has not created a more liberated generation, but rather a much more insecure one.

I worked for seven years in a youth club, and one of the observations I made was this. If we did not have any rules in the club, anarchy reigned, the numbers dropped and the club failed. However, if, in consultation with the young people, we had a set of rules and regulations, we discovered that the club thrived and grew. The reason for this is simple: the young people like to know their boundaries. It gives them great security. They will kick against them and constantly push you on them, but that's exactly what gives them security. Young people need boundaries, and one of these boundaries is to teach them that there is right and wrong.

Step B: Live by the core values that you believe in

Having established our core values, we then need to teach our children how to live by them. Again, the role that parents play in this is crucial. Let me set you an imaginary scenario.

You've got a young child. You go to the supermarket and you come to the checkout points. For once you have a choice of checkouts to queue at. One is operated by a dumpy girl with glasses, the other by a shapely blonde. Which checkout do you join? Do you think it's important, and does it matter? Well, I think it does. If you choose the shapely blonde every time, it conveys a message to two people. First, it communicates to the dumpy girl that she's not as valuable, and second, your child will pick up the hidden message that you treat people differently. Teach your children:

- to value people for who they are, not what they look like or own or have achieved.
- to give people dignity. Buy the *Big Issue*, but even if you can't, try to look the seller in the eye and smile. It does help.
- to treat all people equally, whatever the cost.

Step C: Work out what it means in advance to live by your core values

When I was in college I played a lot of rugby. Part of the culture of rugby is to drink a lot of alcohol. I had decided that one of my core values was not to get drunk. This meant limiting myself to a couple of pints on a night out. However, a subtle pressure could be put on you during the after-game drinks! To survive I needed to learn how to say no and to be confident in asking for a soft drink.

Having helped our children think through and work out their core values, we need to move on and give them other life-skills.

LIFE-SKILL 2: LEARNING HOW TO SOLVE PROBLEMS

Some of my most vivid memories as a child are of my first experience of pain. The time I fell through a plate-glass window, the first time I fell off a swing, the first time I broke a bone. I remember at the age of 8 watching a man die on the beach. He'd been rescued after experiencing difficulties in the sea, but despite all the efforts of the life-guard he died. These were all shocks to me as I'd not experienced real pain until then. There is nothing special in my story, and that is my point. All of it is part of life, and one of the lessons our children need to learn is that life is full of difficulties. The secret in life is not trying to avoid difficulties but, rather, learning how to cope with them. One of the major reasons why young people take drugs is to avoid pain. Part of the reason they take them is that it's the only way they know to cope with the pain. However, what we want to do is to give our children life-skills which show there are other ways of copying with difficulties. We can do this by teaching them some basic facts about decision-making.

Fact 1: Avoid impulsiveness

This is a difficult one because all young people are impulsive. The problem with being impulsive is that it considerably raises the risk stakes. By definition, acting on impulse means you have not thought through all the permutations – hence the risk factor. For young people, taking risks can be great fun, so one of the lessons we can teach our youngsters is that impulsive decisions have consequences. I'm not against people taking risks – in fact they can be a healthy side of life – but young people do need to realize the potential consequences. Now, please hear what I am saying: the only way that young people are going to learn is through making mistakes. The hard part for a parent is first watching them make the mistakes, but also protecting them from the

big mistakes. So, to give an example: smoking one cigarette is a mistake. However, to start smoking two or three
a day is a big mistake, because it is a fast path to
addiction.

Another example: to get drunk is a mistake which I hope
youngsters will learn from. However, suppose your
teenager is at a party. He's drunk three pints, and somebody comes in and says there's a great party on the other
side of town. As he's the only one who can drive, the pressure is now on him to make an impulsive decision. To get
in the car would be a big mistake, to have an accident
could be a tragic one. The hard role you have as a parent
is to help them to avoid the bad impulsive decision.

You can help your children by helping them develop
problem-solving skills.

Fact 2: Learn that saying no can be good!

We live in a world where to say no is considered negative. Well, it can be, but it can also be positive. To say no
to the above drink-driving scenario is a positive decision, to say no to drugs is a positive statement. We need
to teach our children that saying no can be good!

LIFE-SKILL 3: KNOWING THE REAL VALUE OF FRIENDSHIP

Let's go back to our drink-driving analogy. Again, it's the same scenario and they ask your son the same question: 'Come on, you've only had three pints – you can drive us.' Imagine now that one of the group says, 'No, that's unfair to John. We can't ask him to do that. He could lose his licence or, worse, he could kill all of us!' Your son will now find it much easier to make a decision. Your children need to develop friends who will stand by them, who will be there when the going gets tough. The problem is, you can't pick their friends for them – you just have to stand back and let them learn. But you can do two things:

1   The first is always have an open door to their friends. No matter what you think of them, don't close that door. Because if you close that door a number of things will happen. First, you will not stop the friendship; rather, your son or daughter will be more determined to make it work. Second, you will not know what is going on, as you will never see them. Keep that door open.

2   The second thing you can do in this area is to be a good role model. Do you have good friends? Do your children see them laughing and having a good time with you? Do they see them standing by you when you go through difficult times? Demonstrate to them the power of friendship.

ACTION POINTS

- **Spend half an hour considering:**
  your views on authority
  your views on God and spirituality
  your attitude towards health
  your views on sexuality
  the way you treat other people
  your attitude towards money and possessions
  your attitude towards power
  knowing right from wrong
  the way you deal with pain and difficulties.

- **Take time out to consider whether you are effectively passing them on to your children.**

- **Spend time with your children, helping them to see the value of saying no.**

The only way people learn is through making mistakes. One of the goals of a parent is to try and protect their children from the big mistakes.

GOAL 6

TO HELP YOUNG PEOPLE TO ACCEPT RESPONSIBILITY

I remember walking into a room in our youth club and, as I did so, three youngsters rushing out of the other door. As I looked at the point they'd just vacated I saw a lot of graffiti on the wall. To say I was mad would be an understatement! I quickly gathered together the three youngsters and asked them a simple question: 'Who did it?' There was silence; no amount of threats could get them to own up.

I appreciate that the above is typical behaviour of young people down the years. But there has been a major change in our culture in the way it views responsibility. This is brilliantly highlighted by Ben Elton in his book *Popcorn*. In it, he tackles the issue of whether screen violence makes us a more violent society. Near the beginning of the book his main character goes into a speech about what's wrong with our modern world. His friend has just suggested that he is drunk.

'And I shall tell you why I've had a couple,' Bruce answered triumphantly. 'Because I have an addictive personality, that's why. You know how I know? A court told me so. Oh yes it did, when I got busted for drink-driving. That was my plea. That's what I said. Not "I'm sorry your honour, I'm an irresponsible [idiot]," but "I can't help it. I have an addictive personality." I drank the booze, I drove the car but it *wasn't my fault*! I had a problem, you see, and it saved me a prison term ...'

... 'Addicted to sex,' Bruce explained to Dove. 'Did you read that? He said it to *Vanity Fair* after being caught in bed with various ladies to whom he was not married. He said he was addicted to sex. Not just a gutless, cheating little [twerp], you notice. No. A sex addict. He had a problem, so it was *not his fault*.'

... 'Nothing is anybody's fault. We don't do wrong, we have problems. We're victims, alcoholics, sexaholics. Do you know you can be a shopaholic? That's right. People aren't greedy any more, oh, no. They're shopaholics, victims of commercialism. Victims! People don't fail any more. They experience negative success. We are building a culture of gutless, spineless, self-righteous, whining cry-babies who have an excuse for everything and take responsibility for nothing ...'[5]

I have been in youth work long enough to know that people are victims of circumstances. But there are also many who are not. Our problem is that people will not take responsibility for their actions. One of the major roles that parents can play is to teach our young people that actions have consequences, and that they must also take responsibility for those consequences. This can't be done in a couple of days, but rather it's in the way that we teach them to deal with a number of issues they face as they move from childhood into adulthood.

LIFE-SKILL 1: HOW TO HANDLE MONEY

Your children will grow up in a world that will want to throw money at them. Credit cards, store cards, instant loans, overdrafts are all part of modern life. It is easy for any person to visit the high street and get £2,000–£3,000 instant credit. It is vital therefore, that we give our children a real sense of the value of money, to appreciate the true cost of items.

A small but significant way is to give them pocket money and to give them a choice as to what it can be used on. For example, you may give them £6 a week and tell them they can use it on sweets or youth clubs, or save it. It is not for buying clothes. In that small and simple way you have given them some freedom to make choices. It may be that when they get to a certain age you give them a more substantial amount of money, and they are now also responsible for buying their clothes. The point of the exercise is that you are trying to help them learn to budget and realize that if you buy one thing you can't have the other. It is a small but important lesson which will help them on the learning curve of taking responsibility.

LIFE-SKILL 2: HOW TO HANDLE EMOTIONS

As adults we quickly forget the teenage years, but we would do well to remember the emotional side. For this is a period in life when we feel strongly about everything. If we can help our children work through these emotions we will be helping them on the road towards taking responsibility. And I see that there are three characteristics to a young person's life:

- *the circle of emotions* – that is, feeling fine one day and terrible the next. They can be up or they can be down, rarely in between! This can lead to the problem of making decisions based on their impressions – often dangerous!
- *the breaking away* – part of the process of growing up is the need to establish your own independence. This will happen with your children. You need to gently help them establish this. This can be difficult because it needs to happen over a period of time and can cause much tension and tears.
- *the search for identity* – as well as being your son or daughter, your child is also a unique creation. Part of adolescence is discovering who they are.

The problem with all this is that your children do not wake up one morning and simply say, 'I want my independence today' or 'I know who I am.' Rather, it's a gradual exploration, and so an important part you play is to help them as much as possible. You need to do this, or they will find other ways of dealing with all these conflicting emotions, like getting drunk or taking pills to blot out the confusion, even if these are only short-lived.

So you can help by:

- trying to prepare them by talking about it
- giving them a secure space to explore
- always keeping the door open
- and being prepared to be yelled at!

There is a third, final life-skill that is so important that I have given it a separate chapter – so read on.

Drugs were an escape for me. They removed my feelings of insecurity, fear and inadequacy. I didn't know it, but I needed to be surrounded by security and love. All my life I had tried to buy love. I always pretended that I had it.

ACTION POINTS

- If you give your children pocket money, what is it
  for? Make some clear distinctions for them.
  sweets
  CDs
  youth clubs
  clothes

- When you do 'handy jobs' around the house,
  involve your children. Let them do some of the
  jobs and expect them to make mistakes!

- Give them tasks in the home that they are
  responsible for, like walking the dog, cutting the
  grass, helping with the bins.

- Always keep the door open for them.

GOAL 7

TO HELP YOUR CHILDREN LEARN HOW TO HANDLE ALCOHOL

I remember being fascinated as a child by my father drinking wine. As I grew up I recognized that to be an adult meant many things, but one was being able to drink alcohol. So I eagerly awaited the day I could try it. In fact, I remember opening the fridge door and finding an opened bottle of wine. Certain that no one was looking, I took a quick mouthful. The taste was disgusting! I couldn't believe this was the stuff that my father drank.

Children and young people are surrounded by alcohol and advertising for it. The final life-skill we need to give our youngsters is the ability to handle alcohol well. I have given it a whole chapter, not because it is any more important than other life-skills, but rather because we live in a society that perceives alcohol not as a drug but as part of a recreational activity. It is vital that we have a healthy view towards alcohol and that we pass this on to our children. Let me start with two facts.

- A little alcohol is good for the human body.
- The abuse of alcohol is a major factor in many social, emotional and physical conditions.

Having accepted those two facts, we need to teach our children two things. First, that alcohol is a drug, and, second, how best to handle it.

ALCOHOL IS A DRUG

Alcohol abuse kills more people than all other drugs put together.

To help us understand the problems abusing alcohol can cause, read the following statistics:

- 25 per cent of male hospital admissions are alcohol-related.
- Alcohol use is associated with:
    75 per cent of all stabbings
    70 per cent of all beatings
    50 per cent of all domestic violence
    33 per cent of burglaries
    50 per cent of street crime
    85 per cent of crime in pubs and clubs
    44 per cent of all violent assaults
    35 per cent of child abuse cases.

- Half of all incidents of disorderly behaviour in urban areas happen just after the pubs close, mainly on Friday and Saturday nights, usually involving young men.
- Half of all facial injuries in the 15–25 age group happen after the victim or aggressor has been drinking, and usually take place in bars, clubs or in the streets.[6]
- A thousand young people under the age of 15 are admitted to hospital each year with alcohol poisoning. All need emergency treatment.[7]

HOW BEST TO HANDLE IT

You have to decide what your view on alcohol is. If you are somebody who abstains from drinking it, you will need to have clearly thought-out reasons for this and why you would want your children to do likewise. If, however, you are happy to drink in moderation, then you need to help your children to learn this skill. The place it begins is with you and the example you set. If, as a lifestyle, you see the weekends as a time to unwind and regularly get drunk, then do not be surprised if your children grow up following that pattern. However, if you can show your children that you enjoy a drink but that you do so in moderation, you have set a model for them to follow. You then need to let them explore drink in stages. For example, when they are young let them have a sip out of your glass. This will achieve two things. First, it will take away the mystery factor – they will have tasted alcohol. Second, for most children it will be enough, for they will not enjoy it. As they get older, allow them the occasional low-alcohol drink with you at a meal. Then allow them to have a glass of wine. As you can see, a pattern develops which we hope will give them the life-skills to cope with the many pressures that they will face in this area.

PARTY TIME!

The other issue you face is the increasing pressure of drinks at parties. So let me finish by suggesting some practical tips. If the party is in your home, agree some ground rules beforehand:

- no spirits (and make sure you remove your own stock)
- stay around (out of the way, but still in the house)
- have plenty of good food available – bread and pasta for example – so they don't drink on an empty stomach.

If they are going to someone else's party, make sure you know:

- where it is
- how they are getting home (better to give them the money for a taxi if in doubt).

Finally, talk to them about the danger of spiking drinks.

We think it is advertising and promotional materials which affect and influence younger smokers. The tobacco industry needs 300 new smokers a day just to keep level and to replace the smokers who die.[8]

**Take 1,000 young adult males who smoke.
On average this is what will happen to them
in their lifetime:**

**1 will be murdered
6 will be killed on the roads
250 will be killed before their time
by tobacco.**

GOAL 8

TO HELP YOUR CHILDREN STAY TOBACCO-FREE

We rightly get worried about what illegal drugs our children may be offered and may take. However, we often ignore, if not tolerate, the use of legal ones such as tobacco. If you, as a parent, smoke, you will not only have a much harder task in educating your own children not to smoke, but you will also have a problem when talking about illegal drugs to your children. If you tell your children not to smoke cannabis or take Ecstasy they may look at you smoking and wonder – is there any difference? Smoking is a major health risk in our culture and it kills six times more people in the UK than road and other accidents, murder, manslaughter, suicide, illegal drugs and AIDS all put together.

To help us understand the nature of smoking, here are some facts and statistics.

- If you get through 20 a day, over 40 years, you will consume 292,000 cigarettes. That's more than £36,000 up in smoke by 1999 living standards.

- 33 per cent of the British population smoke.
- 25 per cent of 16–19-year-olds smoke.
- It's estimated that tobacco causes over 120,000 early deaths every year in the UK.
- Tobacco-smoking is responsible for more adverse health effects than any other psychoactive drug. The more you smoke, the more likely you are to suffer from heart disease, blood clots, cancer, strokes, bronchitis, bad circulation and ulcers. Pregnant women who smoke a lot tend to have smaller babies, and they run a greater risk of losing their child before or shortly after birth.
- It is clear that there is a link between parents who smoke and illnesses in children.[9]

ACTION POINTS

- Be aware that tobacco is potentially a killer.

- More young girls are smoking because it helps keep weight off. Keep encouraging your daughter that she is loved for who she is.

- Passive smoking could affect your child's health. If you smoke, for your child's sake consider quitting.

- When talking to your children about drugs, always include tobacco and alcohol in the discussion.

- As a parent, your attitude to tobacco is crucial — you need to be clear what you communicate. If you do not disapprove, young people are more likely to smoke.

Try to be to your children what you wished your parents to be to you

SIX GOALS TO HELP
YOU AS A PARENT

GOAL 9

DON'T TAKE ALL THE CREDIT, DON'T TAKE ALL THE BLAME

I enjoy reading self-help books, and I can always put them into two categories. In the first come books which make you feel like giving up after you've read them – they make you feel such a failure. The writer has every intention of helping you, but somehow they just manage to make you feel so inadequate. The second type is when I connect with what the writer is saying, and it lifts my inner being. After I've read the book the world looks a better place, the next-door neighbour's dog doesn't seem so annoying, and above all I feel that there is some hope in what I'm trying to achieve. What is it that makes the difference between the first and second type of book? It is obviously a number of things, but I think that one of the most important is that the second type is written from reality: the books are about joys and pains, about things that worked and others that did not. They are books that do not pretend to have any easy answers, but they do offer hope.

And that is one of my major purposes in writing this book. There are no simple answers to keeping your children drug-free. I wish it were that simple – but it's not. But as we have already seen, there is the possibility of giving them a framework that will give them a greater chance of making it through life without taking drugs.

However, in writing a book like this my purpose is to help you as a parent. And so there is a very important principle that you need to hear. You must realize that you're not a failure as a parent. All your experience may tell you so. Your child still wears nappies whereas your friend's child flushes the toilet after they've used it. Your child manages a monosyllabic grunt while your friend's child can recite the whole works of Shakespeare. It may be that you have teenage children and they don't look the way you'd like them to – rings through nose, ears and lips, whereas your friend's children are simply … smart! But you are not a failure.

On a more serious note, I have sat with many parents as they've poured out their hearts and shared their pain about their children, and at some point they will blurt out, 'Where did we fail?' The answer is that they did not. There is no magic formula for bringing up children. You know what I mean: 'Do A, B and C and your children will work out well-rounded people.' I wish it were so easy! The truth is that each child is a unique creation. There is nobody else like them. To help, I'd like to share three principles with you in the hope that these will take away some of the guilt you may feel as a parent, and make you realize that you are doing a good job after all.

RECOGNIZE THE LIMITS OF YOUR RESPONSIBILITY

It's taken me many years, but I've finally realized we can't make other people do what we want them to. Which parent hasn't wished they could make their son or daughter pick another partner? Who hasn't wished that they could change their son's or daughter's behaviour to something that would be acceptable in front of their friends? The desire to control our children's lives comes from all the best reasons – our desire to see them get the best out of life, a realization that certain decisions could have major implications. But our children will refuse to do what we want, and we can feel the control slipping out of our fingers. We need to let that responsibility go. We can't make decisions for our children. We want to be able to wave a magic wand and make everything all right – but we can't do that. Your children will make decisions that may well result in pain for them.

We need to free them to make their own choices and to learn through the consequences. The role of a parent is to let children make mistakes. That's not bad parenting – that's good parenting. The hard part for a parent is to protect children from making big mistakes. We need to have given them frameworks within which to make decisions. We must just stand with them and love them, irrespective of the decision.

HELP YOUR KIDS STAY DRUG-FREE

REALIZE THE GREAT THINGS YOU HAVE DONE

Many of us will always look at the negative side of things. 'If only I had done this with my children,' or 'If only we had made this decision.' And we go through this whole list and conclude that we are very poor parents. Take five minutes and list all the good things about your children. You've made many good choices, you've created a loving environment for your kids, you've sacrificed many things for them. You are a good parent. Your children may not recognize it yet, but that is not the point. So stop putting yourself down – you're probably doing a good job.

TALK TO SOME GOOD FRIENDS

I think one of the most moving experiences I have had is when I've been carrying some problem for months. It has kept me awake at night, it has made me more touchy, and I seem to lose my temper at very small things. Finally I pluck up the courage to tell a good friend. The relief at just telling the person is great, but imagine the feeling when they tell me that what I've been going through is 'normal' and that loads of people face the same problem. We are created as social creatures and we need the support of friends. One of the most positive steps you can take is to talk through your problems with a good friend. They may not have any answers, but the support you get will help you cope.

People will come home if they know somebody is waiting for them

One thing I have learned is that success is not about money and power. Real success is about relationships. There's no point in making $50 million a year if your teenagers think you're a jerk and you spend no time with your wife.

Christopher Reeve ('Superman')[10]

GOAL 10

TO LISTEN TO WHAT YOUNG PEOPLE ARE SAYING

I was recently leading a sixth-form conference on drug and alcohol abuse. At one point I stopped and asked them a question: 'Imagine that we are able to turn the clock back and that you are 12 again. Having just been through some of the most painful years of your life, what advice would you give to your parents to help you through the teenage years?'

The answers came fast, spoken from the heart and laced with great advice. These five statements came from the young people. We would do well to listen to them.

CREATE TIME FOR US

A friend of mine told me of a medical consultant he knew. This consultant was well respected in his field and was therefore in much demand outside his working hours. He spent long hours in his work and would then often spend the evening giving some lecture or attending a committee. One engagement took him away for four days. On returning he walked into his home as his teenage son was on his way out. 'Did you miss me while I was away?' asked the father. His son's reply cut him to the heart. 'Why should I? You're never home anyway, so what's the difference?'

I tell that story not to make anyone feel guilty, but for us to realize two truths. First, we may think we are spending time with our children but we are probably fooling ourselves about the amount. According to all the surveys, the average father spends around about 4 minutes a day talking to his children. Second, it is obvious from the son's comments that he is hurt. And he's hurt because he desperately wants to spend time with his father and mother, and the fact that they haven't spent time with him has broken him.

You need to understand that children want, and need, time with you, and – here is the strange fact – the older your teenagers get, the more time they need with you. Yes, I did say that: the older they get, the more time they need. The reason for this is obvious. As they get older they face more and more dilemmas every day. They are feeling pressure from all quarters – friends, school, society – and they need somewhere they can take refuge. And that somewhere is you! They need you as a base they can return to, a sheltered harbour, so that when the storm gets too rough they can head back to you. And you have to create time – to make it a priority, above everything else. You watch them play sport, take them out for a coffee, go to the cinema together – anything that creates time for them to build bridges with you. In doing that you are developing opportunities for communication to take place between you and your child.

Some tips for creating time with your children:

- have a weekly activity you do together – going to a football match, shopping, swimming, anything that your child finds fun
- eat your meals together as a family
- surprise them and take them away for a weekend: go camping in the hills or by the beach.

LISTEN TO US

One of the greatest complaints that teenagers make about adults is that 'they ask a question and answer it themselves' or 'we start a conversation but halfway through they interrupt us with their opinion' or 'they say they are listening but it never makes any difference.' In other words, their complaint is that we never listen to them. My observation is that it is a very fair criticism.

I came across a great piece of advice about marriage, but as I read it I realized it was just as valuable for parents and young people.

When a man whose marriage was in trouble sought his advice, the Master said, 'You must learn to listen to your wife.'

The man took his advice to heart and returned after a month to say that he had learned to listen to every word his wife was saying.

Said the Master with a smile, 'Now go home and listen to every word she isn't saying.'[11]

That is great advice. First of all, we need to listen to what our teenagers are saying, and that's not easy to do. It means that we have to create time, and that can often be at a moment when it's not convenient – but we must make the effort. It may be that we create a regular space – we go out for a coffee, go to a regular sports fixture, go shopping. Whatever it is, we are creating an environment where communication can begin to develop. It probably means that we will have to start the conversation, so ask questions such as, 'Tell me, I know it must be hard, but what do you know about drugs?' Then we must give them space to reply – we must listen to their views.

We must also demonstrate that we listen to them by following some of their advice. If we do this it will demonstrate that we respect their opinion, and that is so important to young people. You will not know how much their well-being and worth is lifted when you demonstrably listen to them.

SHARE YOUR MISTAKES WITH US

I have learned in life that what most helps people is not our success stories but rather our stories of pain and failure. In our failure and pain we can build one another up. The reason for this is simple: we all experience a lot of failure, and knowing that someone else has been through the same thing really helps. It may not solve the problem, but it just helps to have someone walk through it with you. So it is true with our teenagers. They find life hard, they make mistakes. What they are saying to you is: tell us what it was like when you were our age. And don't fool yourself. I've lost count of the number of parents who express disappointment that their daughter wants to marry her boyfriend at the age of 20. 'How old were you when you got married?' This is usually followed by a silence, then words to the effect, 'I was 19, but it was different then.' Well, the culture was, but those feelings of love and desire are no different. Now if you were married at 19 and divorced at 26, that's different – you have a story young people want to hear. Share with them your expectations and your pain.

One has to find the right moment and the correct time, but at some point it is good to share our past failures with our teenagers. If we struggled with our parents – share it. If we made mistakes with drugs – share it. You will find that it will build major bridges with your teenagers, and their respect and trust in you will increase. However, in sharing our failures, we need to realize the third comment these teenagers made.

GIVE US THE FACTS

Young people overwhelmingly say that the people they most want advice from is their parents! But it's a special sort of advice – it's advice that gives them all the facts so that they can make informed choices. We can also share our own opinion on the matter, but we must resist the temptation to preach at them. Once we start that, we have lost them. I know this is very hard, but if we have shared our failures we must not use that as emotional blackmail. Give them the facts. Give them your opinion. Then let them make their own minds up. Whatever decision they make, they have to live with the life-long consequence.

LOVE US FOR WHO WE ARE

As we have already seen, this is fundamental. Imagine that we are sitting in your living room and talking about your son or daughter. In the midst of our discussion I ask you to answer one question. Here it is: 'What is the most important question on your teenager's mind?'

Take a minute and think about it. What answer would you give? I'm sure lots of possibilities fly through your mind – exams, career, boy/girlfriends, drugs. All very important issues, but beneath it there is one fundamental question.

The young person may never verbalize it or even consciously acknowledge it, but it is there. This is the question: 'Do you love me?'

Deep down inside every son and daughter that question lurks. In one sense it shapes their whole world. As I spoke with these sixth formers, out came the simple statement: love us for who we are, not what we achieve – great advice. It means that you are creating an environment where your children know that whatever they do, however high they climb or low they fall, you are always there for them. My observation of life is that young people who know that they are loved simply cope with life in a more positive and better way than those who question whether they are loved. It does not mean they are more successful, better-looking, richer – simply that they cope better.

When I was between the ages of about 12 and 21, I could not talk to my father. This was not because he was a violent or an abusive man, or that he set out to make me feel distant from him, or inferior, or weak. In fact he treated me in a way that most onlookers would have regarded as entirely normal. The problem, I realize now, was that he tried to conceal and deny the weaknesses that embarrassed him – shyness, caution, lack of confidence – in such a way that he left no common ground of vulnerability between us, no comfortable space in which I could confess my own weaknesses to him as I might confess them to my mother or my sister.

Richard Benson, editor of *The Face*[12]

ACTION POINTS

- If you do not do this already, make a regular date in your diary and spend time with your children.
- Go and ask their advice about something.
- Next time your son or daughter talks to you, demonstrate to them that what they have to say is important.
- Tell them you love them.

GOAL 11

TO KNOW WHAT AND WHEN TO TELL YOUNG PEOPLE ABOUT DRUGS AND ALCOHOL

Before we look in closer detail at these issues, we need to recognize two truths when dealing with children and young people. If we can accept these we have a chance of building some bridges to communicate our thoughts on these issues.

LESSON 1

Accept the fact that your child is going to do things that you are not happy with. They will wear clothes that shock you. They will choose hairstyles that resemble a cross between a bird's nest and a hedgehog! Some of their friends will not be your choice. Their bedroom will never be as tidy as you want. And you will be exceptionally fortunate if you do not discover them drunk at some point. These will all be major stresses for you, but I would like to suggest that they are also part of the growing-up process. They are the joys and pains of adolescence. The secret and the very hard lesson to learn as a parent is to know your bottom-line issue. The bottom-line issue is the one at which you stand and say, 'This is far enough – no further.' The problem with many parents is that they make the bottom line the wrong issue. I remember talking to a mother of a teenage girl. She was very happy with her daughter's progress in school, but then she said, 'She wants to have her nose pierced with a stud. Well, I've told her she can't.' As she said it, images of major rows and conflict flooded my mind. I simply thought to myself, 'Wrong battle'. You see, if that is made the bottom line, what will the parent do when the child repeatedly comes home drunk? What will you do if you discover your daughter 'popping pills' with her friends? Decide what your bottom-line issues are with your children, and then work backwards in thinking it through.

LESSON 2

Try to remember how you felt about your parents when you were a teenager. How did your parents talk to you? Did it help you, or did you feel they were lecturing you? Try to be to your children what you wished your parents to be to you. It is hard to do but it will be really worth the effort.

WHEN AND WHAT TO SHARE?

This is probably one of the hardest lessons for us to learn, for the simple truth is that there is no set formula for the right time. When to start talking about drugs with your children will vary from family to family, but one thing I am certain of is that the time is earlier than we think or would like it to be. Most parents struggle with the idea of talking about these issues with children under the age of 10, but that is where I think we need to begin. I believe this for a number of reasons:

1   If you have shared your views they will understand why you believe them. This can be done in a very natural way. For example, when they see you taking medicine you can talk to them about the positive side of drugs. Explain to them all the benefits that the advance in medicine has brought to life. But then at the same time begin to explain about the bad side of drugs. Share with them how some of their class-mates might try to offer them something that looks like a sweet. Or there might be someone, perhaps a brother of one of their classmates, who is hanging around after school and offers them some sweet-like substances. If that happens, tell them, do two things. First, don't accept it, and second, come and tell you. It is very important that at this point you communicate to them that when they come to you, no matter what they tell you, you will not be shocked or annoyed (both of which you may feel!). It is essential they know this so that there is always a channel of communication open. Close this channel down and you will not know what is going on in the play-ground.

2   Having made Point 1, the good news is that your children still have some innocence left and are still young enough that, if offered drugs or alcohol, they will come and talk about it with you.

3   By talking to them about drugs and alcohol you can guarantee that the information they are given is accurate. They will receive lots of other information from many different sources, a lot of it good. But if you share it, you know it will all be good.

THE TEENAGE YEARS

As they enter the teenage years your approach has to change. By now their horizons are widening and they are getting information from many different sources. This is a good thing, but it makes your task a bit harder because they are now developing their own ideas on issues. So how and when you talk with them is very important. You must also realize that the advice and influence of their friends is becoming much more important to them. This is why I spent a couple of chapters on life-skills, because this is the age they really need them. Here are some ways we can raise the issues of drugs with our children. But first, before you can do anything, you must realize a truth.

No area of Britain is untouched by drugs and the children in your son's or daughter's school can get anything they want. If we fail to accept this it will be very hard to tackle the problem. We have to face up to the reality of the wide and easy availability of drugs.

Ask questions

Have a cup of coffee with your daughter or son and talk with them about the issues. Now please note, I said *with* them, not *to* them. One of the questions you could ask is what their friends' views on drugs are, and remember, you must not react to what they tell you. If you do, the chances are that they will not talk about it again with you. What you need to do is discuss it with them. Remember the chapter on listening to your teenagers? What these young people are saying is that they want openness and honesty and all the facts, so that's where you start. Don't say, 'Listen, honey, I know you think we are old and out of touch, but we know that drugs are bad and don't work. We love you, so please don't do it.' What she thinks is, 'You're right, you are old and out of touch, because I know drugs are fun.' Rather, you begin, 'I understand that it's hard with all your mates, and I know they seem to have a good time – but tell me what you know about drugs, tell me what you've learned.' Then your discussion has started; the lines of communication are open.

Your attitude to drink and drugs

As you talk with your son or daughter, explain your views on drugs and alcohol. Tell them how you set your standards for drinking, what you think is an acceptable level for you. Share with them how you came to that conclusion. Do you have drink at home? Explain to them why. What is your policy on them drinking alcohol with you? Again, explain why. As you talk the issues through with your children, gently share with them your views on the topic. Share your concerns about excessive alcohol and drug abuse. Try not to get into lecturing mode!

Good news!

Tell them the good news. While everybody talks about the number of young people who take drugs, remind them that over 70 per cent say no to drugs. Talk to them about how they can learn to say no. Share with them how they can cope with the friends who may be pressurizing them to take drugs. As we know, one of their fears will be that if they say no to their friends they will be excluded from the group. Explain that saying no means they are in the majority – they will be still part of the 'in' crowd. It may also be a good time for them to learn that true friends stick with you, and don't desert you when the going gets tough.

Prescribed medicines

When you or your child are prescribed medicine, you must ensure that they know there are safe and unsafe amounts to take. Again, this may lead to an opportunity to discuss the subject. If you are taking regular medication (which is a different issue) share why you take it, otherwise if you lecture your children on drugs while at the same time regularly taking prescribed drugs they will get the message that one rule is for them, one rule is for you.

Schools

I also think you should be aware what and when your school teaches on drugs. You can find this out by simply contacting the school and getting their drugs policy and your child's timetable. On the days that they have the drug education, try and start a discussion with your child about what they have learned.

An important lesson we need to learn is that part of the adolescent's experience is to explore. It is a natural part of growing up – so if your child is fairly positive in their comments about drugs, try not to panic, for it probably is just that adolescent exploration phase. At this point what they need is facts, not lectures, so just share your views on the issues.

Vulnerable moments

We also need to be aware of the vulnerable moments in our children's lives, because that's when they will be more open to the pressures to take drugs.

I've highlighted some issues that cause stress for young people:

- moving to a new school – either from primary to secondary, or a move to a new school
- exam time
- you move area because of work
- parents' marital difficulties.

ACTION POINTS

- **Pick up a health education leaflet on drug, alcohol and substance abuse from your local surgery or library.**

- **Remember, shock tactics won't work – so don't try them on your children.**

- **Find out what and when your school teaches on drugs.**

- **Talk to your children about what they have learned in school about drugs.**

- **Look out for those vulnerable moments in your child's life.**

- **If you haven't got a view on your personal use of drugs and alcohol – get one!**

GOAL 12

THERE IS ALWAYS HOPE

I have written this book primarily for parents who are looking for advice about how best to keep their children off drugs. In the chapters preceding this I have tried to provide just that. However, I'm also aware that you could be a parent who has one or two further questions. First, you're certain none of your children are taking drugs, but what are some of the signs you can look out for just to make sure? Chapter 13 deals with this issue.

Second, you've discovered they are taking drugs – what can you do? We'll look at this in Chapter 14.

But in answer to these questions, the first thing I want to say is that there is always hope. If your son or daughter is taking drugs it is probably the most painful experience of your life. But there is hope. Taking drugs does not mean they are an addict. And if they are, you must not believe the myth that says 'once an addict always an addict'. That is clearly not true. There are countless alcoholics, who, a day at a time, have given up alcohol. There are many addicts who have kicked their habit at many of the well-run residential treatment centres. Do not think that because your child is addicted that it's the end of the road – it is not. There is hope.

The next few pages are written just to help you realize that there is hope and a way forward. But one thing is clear: you will need more help than you can get from a book. So at the end of this book there is a page of contact names and telephone numbers for you to make a start.

GOAL 13

HOW TO SPOT IF YOUR CHILD IS USING DRUGS

Obviously our hope is that our children will never regularly take drugs. But if we are worried that they might be, what are the signs we need to recognize? This is difficult, and to explain why, let me tell you a story about a youth worker.

One night on television there was a programme on young people and drugs. The following morning the youth worker's phone did not stop ringing as worried parents called him. A typical conversation went as follows. 'John, I think my son, Dave, is taking drugs.'

Naturally, the youth worker asked the caller why she had come to this conclusion.

'Well,' the mother answered, 'on the television programme they gave some indicators for spotting drug use. One of them was sudden mood swings. Dave has been very moody of late.'

The youth worker tried to reassure her that Dave was not taking drugs.

'But,' she went on, 'they also talked about isolation. About youngsters who spend too much time in their bedrooms and don't talk to their parents. John, Dave comes home every day and after a piece of toast he goes straight to his bedroom.'

No matter how hard John tried, he could not convince her that her fears were misplaced.

That story illustrates why I'm reluctant to write about signs of drug use, because many of the behaviour patterns you are looking for are very similar to 'normal' teenage growth pains. So, for example, mood swings can be a part of 'normal' teenage behaviour. Which parent has not sat utterly confused when one day your daughter is all over you and very warm, and the next day she treats you like some outcast? It's all part of the joys of dealing with someone growing up. However, radical mood swings can also be a sign of drug use. So in trying to look at this issue there are two major dangers: either you read every little sign as an indicator of drug use, or you fail to pick up any of the signs. To help, I have divided the potential indicators of drug use into two categories, emotional and physical.

I think it's worth remembering at this stage that most people view alcohol as recreation and not as a drug. So while parents are looking for signs of drug abuse they miss their child's increasing dependency on alcohol. I would suggest that if your 16-year-old son or daughter is on regular alcohol binges, you need to start to act. More people die and face illness through alcohol abuse than from taking drugs.

EMOTIONAL SIGNS OF DRUG ABUSE

What you are looking for is emotional changes in behaviour that are out of the ordinary. So, for example, if your child has a history of being moody then I would suggest you are looking for some sort of change in their mood pattern. Personalities can be changed by drugs and alcohol. For example:

- Alcohol can make a person more aggressive or more funny than normal.
- Drugs which stimulate will excite a person. So for this you will look for significant changed sleeping patterns, bursts of energy and then periods where they seem overtired for no apparent reason. Hallucinogens will make them paranoid, while depressants will make them sleepy and possibly cause them to have slurred speech.

Is their attention span much shorter than normal? Are they getting stressed over little things? Physical signs can be more obvious, and we will look at those next.

PHYSICAL SIGNS OF DRUG ABUSE

These are some of the signs you are looking for:

- Eating habits are becoming very erratic.
- The mouth and nose are becoming blotchy and red.
- The pupils of the eyes are more dilated or constricted than usual.
- You find remains of cigarette ends or 'joints'.
- You smell strong, sweet, aromatic, smoky smells.
- You notice that your child's breath smells of alcohol on a regular basis.
- You discover needles and syringes in the house.

Even more disturbing is the realization that there is never the amount of money that you thought was in your purse. At first you put it down to forgetfulness or think your partner has taken some small change. But it begins to happen too regularly. Then you notice that certain small personal items seem to be missing. You're not certain how long they have been missing because you hardly use them. Finally, you come home and discover that you have been burgled. But the police are puzzled because it looks as if someone has broken in from the inside. All these examples illustrate the point that if your children are taking drugs they need to pay for them. At first they will ask for more pocket money, but this can never be enough and in desperation they will resort to stealing from their own family.

Of course, many parents will not pick up the signs. This is not because they are bad parents, but rather because it's either such an alien culture or, more obviously, because your son or daughter does not want you to find out! So the day may arise when you are confronted with the reality. How to cope with this is dealt with in the next chapter.

I didn't know how I'd react when I discovered my daughter was taking drugs. I wasn't prepared for this. Would I be angry, like you are with a 4-year-old who gets lost in the supermarket and you spank them out of fear when you find them? But when I saw her I just held her close and cuddled her, and she cried. I didn't judge her. All that mattered to me was that she should survive and know that, whatever she did and whatever happened, I'd be there for her.[13]

GOAL 14

HELP! I THINK MY CHILD IS TAKING DRUGS

Mary's parents had no warning, no time to come to terms with it. Only a few days before they had been telling the next-door neighbours how proud they were of their daughter. They'd just got the news that she had been accepted at Oxford University to read history. They knew it did not make Mary any better than other girls, but secretly they were delighted. Sure, like any parents they had rows with Mary, but she was a good girl. Her new boyfriend seemed so polite, and her Saturday job at Marks and Spencer meant she had money to spend on herself.

The policeman at the front door was a surprise, which quickly turned to shock as they heard what he had to say. Their daughter had been arrested the previous night for 'causing a disturbance of the peace'. But that was not the news that caused their life to spiral out of control. No, it was the small number of Ecstasy tablets she was carrying in her purse that caused the mother to gasp and start crying.

For many parents, there are few worse feelings than discovering that your child is taking drugs. The sheer feeling of helplessness and of despair is beyond measure. There could be an overwhelming feeling of failure and loss of control. These are all normal responses to what you are going through. But do realize that, no matter how you feel, there is hope. These are three steps which I hope will help in the situation.

DON'T PANIC!

Everything inside you will want to. Try to take some deep breaths. You will be overwhelmed by many different emotions: failure, anger, despair, hope. They will all be part of your life for the short-term future. You must learn not to deny them, but rather to deal with them. But what is very important for helping your children is that you go on loving them. You must try not to lash out and say things which may, in the short term, make you feel better but which could do lasting damage. What you must try to do is say reassuring things to your child. This is one of their most vulnerable moments and they do not need a lecture: they simply need to know that you will stick with them. Your reaction at this point can either build or destroy bridges to your children. What is essential is that you build a bridge, because in time they will want to walk across and talk to you.

GO TO A FRIEND AND GET TALKING

We are social creatures, which simply means we need one another. One of the ironies of life is that, faced with a major crisis, we tend to internalize it and never tell anyone. While this is understandable, it is the worst way of dealing with the problem. We need to share our difficulties, either with close and trusted friends or with a professional like a counsellor, doctor or priest. To get through this dilemma you are going to need help. You will need someone to pour out your heart to. As I said before, you will have all these conflicting emotions and you will need to get them out. A good friend you can sit down with is invaluable. They probably will not have any answers, but you're not really looking for that – you just need to talk. If you are worried about what they will think, don't be. They are friends, and that's what they are there for.

REALIZE THAT ALL OF THIS WILL TAKE TIME

Unfortunately, the nature of drug and alcohol abuse is that there are no short-term answers. It will be a long road to recovery – but they can and will break free. So do not make any quick decisions. Rather, you need to establish a number of facts.

1 *Do they want help?* If you've discovered that your child is taking drugs, or even if they have told you, it does not necessarily mean they want help. It is

crucial that they do. If they do not want help, there is little you can do at this stage. If they do want help, then that is a major step towards recovery. But remember, we are talking about a lengthy time, so don't put false expectations on yourself or your son or daughter.

2   *If they don't want help, please don't give up.* You must keep talking to them, or, if they have moved out, keep in touch. Keep on loving them even if they do not want to stop. The time will come when they will want to stop, and you will need the lines of communication open so that they can ask for help.

3   *If they do want help then you need to seek professional advice.* This can be done through many counselling services or with your local doctor. It is something that will need professional help, so as soon as your son or daughter is ready – get it.

4   *Part of demonstrating that you love them means that you learn to trust them again.* This will be hard, but it must be done as it's part of the healing process. However, you need to be wise about the trust – you must not lend them money, whatever they say. If they need something, go and buy it with them. You will also need to be firm and set out the rules. For example, if they are an alcoholic then you have a 'no alcohol in the house' rule for everybody, including yourself.

It will be hard, it will take time, but it is possible to come off drugs. Your son and daughter do not have to stay dependent – there is hope.

FINAL TIME OUT

FIVE DON'TS

- Don't give up on your children.
- Don't underestimate the power of their peers.
- Don't use scare tactics.
- Don't panic when everything seems to be going wrong.
- Don't give up on your children's friends.

FIVE DO'S

- Do tell them you love them.
- Do take time to listen to your children.
- Do tell them about your failures.
- Do give them a hug each day.
- Do build them up.

EPILOGUE: THEY WILL COME HOME

Well, we've made it to the end. For some of you it has been a very painful journey. Sadly, there is no other way to deal with these issues. But, to help, I would like to finish with a story – I hope it encourages you.

Mark was your average teenager. If he had had his time over again he would have made university and got a degree. The reason he didn't is simple: one day he accepted a pill from his friends. He knew all the facts about drugs, but he simply thought, 'Why not?' So he took it, and he had a great time. 'Everybody was wrong after all,' he thought, and that's how he started.

His parents truly loved Mark and so were devastated the day they found out. After their initial panic they began trying to talk with him. They reassured him of their love and wanted to help. 'You must talk to somebody,' they suggested. But by now Mark was mainlining, and he just laughed at them. 'What do you know about anything?' was one of his favourite sayings. His parents kept trying, but he just would not listen.

Finally, he came home one day and simply said that he was leaving. No reason, no thank-yous, just a quick few words and he was off. His parents pleaded with him, but it was to no avail. The last words as he left rang in his ears, 'We will always be here for you.'

The parents were devastated; the first few days they did not sleep and for the first few weeks they thought he would walk back in through the door. But the days turned to weeks, and then to months, and finally years. They never gave up hope, but hearing nothing was hard.

Fifteen years later, there was a knock on the door, and as the mother opened it she instantly knew – her son had come home.

I recently spoke to the father, and as he got to the end of the story a smile filled his face and with tears in his eyes, he simply said, 'They will come home, Paul, they will come home.'

To many of you who are struggling, I share those words to encourage. To encourage you not to give up, but also to encourage you to go on giving your child unconditional love. Because it is unconditional love that is the megaphone that shouts to your children, 'We will always be here for you.' If they know that one truth, they will come home. It may take years, but they will come home.

I hope that through this book I have shown two things: first, that there are no easy answers, but second, that there is always hope. And my desire is that you know that. So don't give up, keep on going and, no matter how dark it may feel at the moment, remember:

They will come home.

HELPLINES

ADFAM National   0171 928 8900
Provides confidential support and an information help-
line for families and friends of drug users. Monday–
Friday 10 a.m.–5 p.m.

The National Drugs Helpline   0800 77 66 00
Offers free and confidential advice about drugs all day,
every day, and can refer you on to local drugs and family
support.

Families Anonymous   0171 498 4680
Operates self-help groups around the country for fami-
lies and friends of people with drug-related problems.
Monday–Friday 1 p.m.–5 p.m.

Welsh Drug and Alcohol Unit   01222 66 77 66
Provides national policy advice and up-to-date information on services in Wales.

Alcoholics Anonymous   0171 833 0022
Every day 10 a.m.–10 p.m.

Scottish Council on Alcohol   0141 333 9677
Provides self-help material and co-ordinates a network
of local agencies providing confidential counselling for
individuals and their families in Scotland.

REFERENCES

1 Paul Merson, *Paul Merson: Rock Bottom*, Blooms-bury, 1995.

2 *Sunday Times*, 5 April 1998, p. 3.

3 *Daily Mirror*, 2 January 1997, p. 33.

4 'Homogeneity of cigarette smoking within peer groups: influence or selection?' *Health Education and Behaviour*, December 1997.

5 Ben Elton, *Popcorn*, Pocket Books, 1997, pp. 82, 83.

6 Dr Patrick Dixon, *The Truth About Drugs*, Hodder and Stoughton, 1998.

7 *A Parent's Guide to Drugs and Alcohol*, Health Education leaflet, 1998, p. 5.

8 Melanie McFadyean, *Drug Wise*, Icon Books, 1997, p. 145.

9 Royal College of Physicians, *Health or Smoking?*, Pitman, 1986.

10 *Sunday Times Magazine*, 6 December 1998.

11 Anthony de Mello, *One-Minute Wisdom*, Doubleday Image, 1985.

12 *Guardian*, 'G2', 15 December 1997, p. 2.

13 Melanie McFadyean, *Drug Wise*, Icon Books, 1997, p. 10.

*Also by Paul Francis and available from HarperCollins*Publishers:

Teenagers: the Parents' One Hour Survival Guide

Do you know what really makes your teenager tick? Do you understand the pressures that teenagers face today? *The Parents' One Hour Survival Guide* shows you how you can help your children cope and offers practical advice on likely problems.

- Talking honestly about sex, drugs and rock 'n' roll – or rap, jungle and acid
- What to do if you find your teenagers are drinking or having under-age sex
- Why teenagers often say, 'My parents don't love me'

One hour with this book could help you and your teenagers survive the coming years. Take time to read – make time to help.

'I have sometimes sneaked into the back of an auditorium and sat enthralled as Paul Francis has spoken to hundreds of teens on this issue. I'm delighted that he's now addressing parents. This book can make a difference to your child.' Rob Parsons